The
Solar System
and Beyond

Our Sun

by Kristine Carlson Asselin

Consultant:
Dr. Ilia I. Roussev
Associate Astronomer
Institute for Astronomy
University of Hawaii at Manoa

CAPSTONE PRESS
a capstone imprint

Fact Finders are published by Capstone Press,
151 Good Counsel Drive, P.O. Box 669, Mankato, Minnesota 56002.
www.capstonepub.com

 Books published by Capstone Press are manufactured with paper
containing at least 10 percent post-consumer waste.

Library of Congress Cataloging-in-Publication Data
Asselin, Kristine Carlson.
 Our sun / by Kristine Carlson Asselin.
  p. cm.—(Fact finders. The solar system and beyond)
 Includes bibliographical references and index.
 Summary: "Describes the Sun, including its place in the galaxy, solar weather, and its affect
on Earth"—Provided by publisher.
 ISBN 978-1-4296-5393-0 (library binding)
 ISBN 978-1-4296-6238-3 (paperback)
 1. Sun—Juvenile literature. I. Title. II. Series.
 QB521.5.A87 2011
 523.7—dc22   2010026024

Editorial Credits
Jennifer Besel, editor; Heidi Thompson, designer; Eric Manske, production specialist

Photo Credits
Capstone Press: 10, 21, 26; iStockphoto: Georgios Kollidas, 4 (inset), Jeremy Mayes, 25; Marilyn Moseley
LaMantia, modified by Capstone, 27; NASA, ESA, and Martino Romaniello (European Southern
Observatory, Germany), 8–9 (background); NASA/JPL-Caltech, 6–7; Photo Researchers, Inc: Science
Source, 3; Photodisc, 23; Shutterstock: Dmitriy Eremenkov, 20–21; SOHO, cover, 1, 5, 8 (inset), 13, 15, 17,
18, 28–29

Artistic Effects
iStockphoto: appleuzr, Dar Yang Yan, Nickilford

Printed in the United States of America in Stevens Point, Wisconsin.
092010   005934WZS11

Table of Contents

Chapter 1

Our Very Own Star

Since ancient times, people have watched and wondered about the Sun. They used it to track changes in the seasons. Many cultures worshiped the Sun like a god. People did not understand the science, but it was impossible for them to ignore the Sun's effect on daily life.

Ancient people also believed Earth was the center of the universe. They were sure the Sun **revolved** around Earth. But in 1543, astronomer Nicolaus Copernicus made a discovery. He claimed that the Sun did not revolve around Earth. Instead, Earth moved around the Sun. Copernicus' discovery changed the way people thought about Earth, the Sun, and the universe.

Nicolaus Copernicus

revolve: to move around an object in space

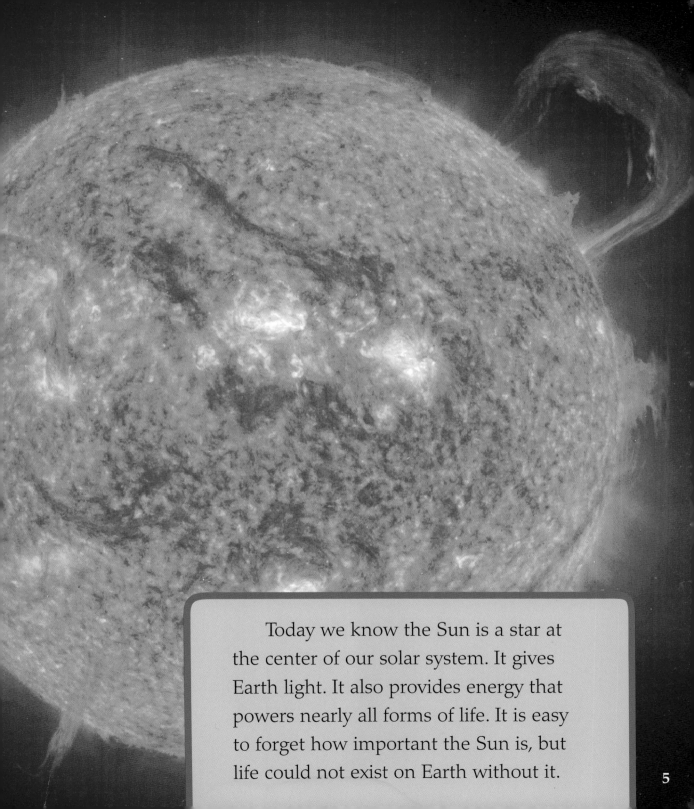

Today we know the Sun is a star at the center of our solar system. It gives Earth light. It also provides energy that powers nearly all forms of life. It is easy to forget how important the Sun is, but life could not exist on Earth without it.

A Place in Space

Our Sun makes its home in the Milky Way **galaxy**. The Milky Way is just one of billions of galaxies in the universe. The Milky Way is a spiral galaxy. Several arms made of dust clouds spread out from the center. New stars are being created all the time in these dark clouds.

galaxy: a large group of stars and planets

Sagittarius Arm

Far 3kpc Arm

Galactic Bar

Long Bar

Near 3kpc Arm

Outer Arm

Perseus Arm

Orion

⊙ Sun

m-Centaurus Arm

The Sun is about 25,000 **light-years** from the center of the Milky Way. It's located in a spiral arm called Orion. The Sun and all other stars orbit around the center of the galaxy. The Sun doesn't move very fast, though. It takes about 250 million years to go around the galaxy once.

light-year: a unit used to measure distance in space; 1 light-year equals about 6 trillion miles (9.5 trillion kilometers)

270

How It Compares

There are hundreds of billions of stars in the universe. Our Sun is just one of those stars. The Sun was born about 4.6 billion years ago. That's a long time for people, but not so long for stars. The Sun is really in the middle of its life.

The Sun is a medium-sized star. It looks bigger to us than other stars. But that's because the Sun is the closest star to Earth. Many stars in the universe are both bigger and brighter than our Sun.

Earth compared to the Sun

Earth is part of a solar system that moves around the Sun. But our solar system is not the only one in the universe. Not every star has planets revolving around it, but many do.

Compared to other stars, the Sun isn't really extraordinary. But the Sun is special because it makes life possible on Earth. The Sun is just the right distance away, making the planet not too cold or hot. As far as anyone knows, the Sun is the only star that supports life.

Closest Stars to Earth

Star Name	Distance from Earth
Sun	93 million miles (150 million kilometers)
Alpha Centauri (a system of three stars)	4.3 light-years
Barnard's Star	6 light-years
Wolf 359	7.7 light-years
BD +36 degrees 2147	8.2 light-years
Luyten 726-8 (a system of two stars)	8.4 light-years
Sirius (a system of two stars)	8.6 light-years
Ross 154	9.4 light-years
Ross 248	10.4 light-years
Epsilon Eri	10.8 light-years

Sun

Mercury

Venus

Moon

Earth

Mars

Asteroid Belt

Ceres
(dwarf planet)

Jupiter

Saturn

Uranus

Neptune

Pluto
(dwarf planet)

Eris
(dwarf planet)

Hold It Together

Along with Earth, the Sun holds seven other planets and their moons in its gravity. The Sun's gravity also pulls in at least five dwarf planets, thousands of asteroids, and trillions of comets. Everything in the solar system revolves around the Sun. The Sun is able to hold all the pieces of the solar system together because it's so big. The Sun is bigger than everything else in the solar system combined. And the bigger the object, the more powerful its gravity.

To get a better idea of the Sun's size, imagine the Sun is a ball that's the size of a small car. In this mini solar system, Earth is a bit smaller than a golf ball. It is more than three football fields away from the Sun. Jupiter is a little larger than a basketball and is about a mile (1.6 km) away. Pluto is a pea, 7 miles (11 km) from the Sun.

FACT: If the Sun was hollow, more than 1 million Earths would fit inside.

gravity: a force that pulls objects together

Chapter 2

A Hot Ball of Gas

Standing on Earth, the Sun looks like a fiery ball in the sky. In reality, it is made almost entirely of hot hydrogen gas called plasma. The temperature at the Sun's core is about 28 million degrees Fahrenheit (16 million degrees Celsius). The heat fuses hydrogen atoms into helium. This process, called nuclear fusion, creates the energy that will keep the Sun burning for billions of years.

The Sun's size is the result of a balancing act inside the star. Pressure from the Sun's hot gas pushes against the Sun's gravity. The powerful gravity pulls the gas toward the core, keeping the Sun from blowing apart.

FACT: When an object gets hotter, its color changes from red to white. Scientists watch changes in the Sun's color to estimate its temperature.

core: the inner part of a star

The Sun's surface is called the photosphere. The light we see comes from this layer of the Sun. The average temperature of the surface is only about 10,000°F (5,500°C). Here's why.

The Sun's light energy is created in its core. The energy then has to travel through miles of matter. It takes thousands of years for the energy to reach the surface. When it finally gets to the top, the energy has cooled millions of degrees.

convective zone

photosphere

radiative zone

core

The inside of the Sun has three zones. Energy is created in the core. Then energy travels through the radiative and convective zones on its way to the surface.

Just like Earth, the Sun has an **atmosphere**. It is made up of two layers above the photosphere called the chromosphere and the corona. These layers are thousands of miles wide. They are also very hot and explosive. In the corona, the average temperature is about 4 million°F (2.2 million°C). Scientists do not know why the layers above the photosphere are hotter, not cooler.

The corona is so hot that the Sun's gravity can't keep it all pulled in. Plasma from the corona stretches millions of miles past Earth. It streams away in giant gusts. This escaping plasma is called solar wind. Solar wind blows toward Earth at 250 to 500 miles (400 to 800 km) per second.

photosphere

chromosphere

corona

atmosphere: the gases that surround a planet or star

FACT: Compared to the surface, the corona and the chromosphere are very faint. You can only see them with special instruments or when the Moon passes directly between Earth and the Sun, creating a solar eclipse.

Earth

solar wind

Chapter 3

Solar Weather

We know all about the changing weather on Earth—wind, rain, snow. But did you know the Sun has its own type of weather?

Dark shape-changing sunspots are the most common features of the Sun's weather. Sunspots are areas where **magnetic fields** have broken through the Sun's surface. Viewed safely through a special lens, sunspots look like freckles on the face of the Sun. The spots are cooler than areas around them and appear darker against the surface. These spots warn scientists that the Sun might produce more violent types of weather.

magnetic field: the space near a magnetic body where magnetic forces are detected

Sending up Flares

Solar flares are examples of the Sun's violent weather. Solar flares are flashes of energy that explode from the Sun's atmosphere. One solar flare in 2003 gave off enough energy to power Earth for 1,000 years! Flares can last a few minutes to a few hours. Scientists believe they are caused by magnetic fields crashing into each other. Imagine a gigantic lightning storm!

solar flare

Sun Volcano

A coronal mass ejection (CME) is a powerful solar explosion. It's like a volcano erupting on Earth. A CME erupts from the gases in the corona. A single ejection spews up to 20 billion tons (18 billion metric tons) of plasma into space. A CME will often trigger a solar flare beneath it.

Effects from the Sun's Weather

Dozens of flares and CMEs happen every year on the Sun. Solar wind is always blowing. Lucky for people, Earth is surrounded by a magnetic field. This magnetosphere acts like bubble wrap around a package. It protects Earth from harmful material thrown into space by the Sun.

Solar storms do affect Earth, though. These storms release so much energy they can disrupt power stations and radio signals. Outside the protective magnetosphere, satellites and spacecraft can be damaged or destroyed by solar storms.

The effects of the Sun's weather aren't always bad. The beautiful aurora borealis, or northern lights, are the result of these storms. Particles from the Sun move through the magnetosphere, bumping into atoms in Earth's atmosphere. When the atoms settle down, they release light. This light in the sky is called an aurora.

Chapter 4

Helping Earth

The Earth and Sun share a unique relationship. The Sun is the perfect distance from Earth. If it were a tiny bit closer, Earth would be too hot. If the Sun were a bit farther away, Earth would be too cold for life as we know it. Every human relies on the Sun to provide the light, warmth, and energy needed to survive.

Day and Night

The Sun continuously provides sunlight to Earth. If Earth stood still, only the side facing the Sun would get light. The other side would be cold and dark. But Earth is not still. It spins completely around once every 24 hours. This movement gives the Sun a chance to light the whole planet part of every day.

Day and Night on Earth

night

day

Seasons

While Earth spins, it also **orbits** the Sun. Earth's orbit is oval-shaped. That means the planet isn't the same distance from the Sun at all times. So you'd think it would be winter when Earth is farthest from the Sun's heat. But that's not how it works for the whole planet. Here's why.

Earth doesn't point straight up and down. The planet's **axis** is tilted 23½ degrees. When nearest to the Sun, the northern half of Earth is tipped away from the heat. So it's winter in the Northern Hemisphere—even though the planet is as close to the Sun as it gets. At the same time, the Southern Hemisphere is pointed toward the Sun. It's summer there.

When the planet is at its farthest point in its orbit, the opposite happens. The northern half is pointed toward the Sun, having summer. The southern half is tipped away for a cool winter.

orbit: the path an object follows as it goes around the Sun

axis: an imaginary line that runs through the middle of a planet

Earth's Changing Seasons

Vernal Equinox
Incoming sunlight is equal in both hemispheres.

23½°

Sun

Summer Solstice
Incoming sunlight is greatest in Northern Hemisphere.

Winter Solstice
Incoming sunlight is greatest in Southern Hemisphere.

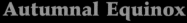

Autumnal Equinox
Incoming sunlight is equal in both hemispheres.

FACT: It takes Earth 365 days to make one complete orbit of the Sun. That's why a year on Earth is 365 days long.

The Water Cycle

Earth's water is in constant motion. It changes from liquid to gas to ice and back again. Without the water cycle, life on Earth would not survive.

The Sun has been responsible for the water cycle on Earth for more than a billion years. The cycle starts when the Sun heats the ocean. Heat causes the water to **evaporate**, changing into a gas called vapor. The vapor rises until cooler temperatures change it into tiny water droplets. The droplets clump together to form clouds. Inside clouds, water droplets mix with dust. When the droplets are too heavy for the clouds to hold, they fall as rain or snow. Eventually the water flows back to the ocean. Then the water cycle begins again.

evaporate: changing into a gas

Earth's Water Cycle

3. The water falls back to Earth as rain or snow.

2. The water vapor cools and forms clouds.

4. The water flows into rivers and, eventually, back to the ocean.

1. The Sun's heat causes the water to evaporate.

Photosynthesis

Light from the Sun is needed to make the air we breathe. The process that makes oxygen is called photosynthesis. And without it, humans couldn't survive.

Photosynthesis starts with plant life. All plants contain chlorophyll, the substance that makes them green. Chlorophyll absorbs sunlight. Then plants turn the energy from sunlight into sugar. They use the sugar for energy, which helps them grow. As the plants make sugar, they release oxygen.

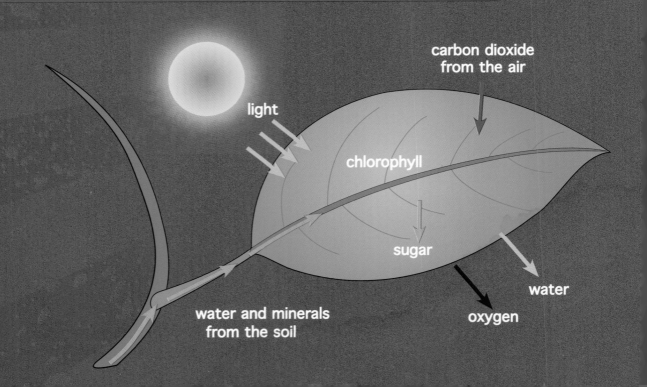

light

carbon dioxide
from the air

chlorophyll

sugar

water

water and minerals
from the soil

oxygen

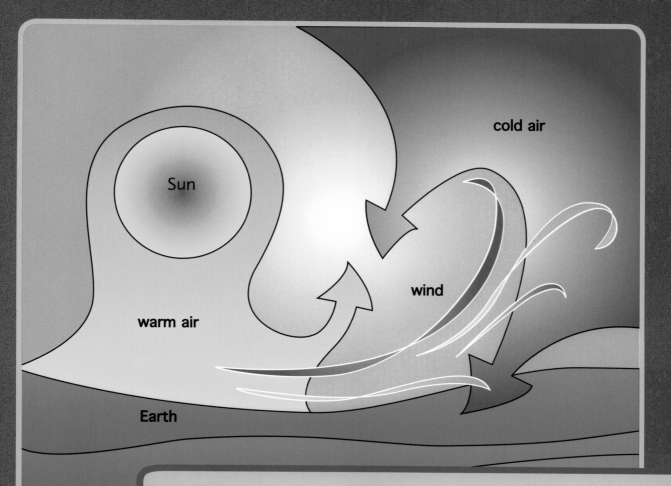

Sun

cold air

warm air

wind

Earth

Wind

The Sun helps create wind too. Air is heated by the Sun. But because of Earth's bumpy land, the air can't absorb the Sun's heat evenly. So some places are warm and others are cool. In the warm spots, the air expands and rises. When the warm air rises, cool air moves in to take its place. This movement creates wind.

Chapter 5

Superstar!

Scientists don't know everything about the Sun, but they are learning new things all the time. Some are measuring its magnetic field activity. This data may help researchers predict solar storms and other activity on the Sun. With this information scientists can make sure astronauts are safer in space. They may also be able to keep electronic systems on Earth from being interrupted.

Closer to home, engineers continue to work to use the Sun's energy for power. One second of the Sun's full energy could power the world for 5,000 years. But humans cannot yet capture all that power. Today solar panels absorb some of the Sun's energy and change it to electricity. The Sun could one day power all our homes.

The Sun—our very own star. It makes plants grow and turns ocean water into rain. It heats air into wind and affects the seasons. The Sun makes our lives possible here on Earth.

Glossary

atmosphere (AT-muh-sfeer)—the layer of gases that surrounds some dwarf planets, planets, moons, and stars

axis (AK-sis)—an imaginary line that runs through the middle of a dwarf planet, planet, or moon; a planet spins on its axis

core (KOR)—the inner part of a dwarf planet, planet, or star

evaporate (i-VA-puh-rayt)—the action of a liquid changing into vapor or a gas; heat causes water to evaporate

galaxy (GAL-uhk-see)—a large group of stars and planets

gravity (GRAV-uh-tee)—a force that pulls objects together; gravity increases as the mass of objects increases or as objects get closer

light-year (LITE-yihr)—a unit for measuring distance in space; a light-year is the distance that light travels in one year

magnetic field (mag-NE-tik FEELD)—the space near a magnetic body or current-carrying body in which magnetic forces can be detected

orbit (OR-bit)—the path an object follows as it goes around a dwarf planet, planet, or star

revolve (ri-VOLV)—to keep turning in a circle around an object

Read More

Asselin, Kristine Carlson. *Stars*. The Solar System and Beyond. Mankato, Minn.: Capstone Press, 2011.

Capaccio, George. *The Sun*. Space! New York: Marshall Cavendish Benchmark, 2010.

James, Lincoln. *The Sun: Star of the Solar System*. Our Solar System. New York: Gareth Stevens Pub., 2011.

Sparrow, Giles. *Destination the Sun*. Destination Solar System. New York: PowerKids Press, 2010.

Internet Sites

FactHound offers a safe, fun way to find Internet sites related to this book. All of the sites on FactHound have been researched by our staff.

Here's all you do:

Visit *www.facthound.com*

Type in this code: 9781429653930

Check out projects, games and lots more at
www.capstonekids.com

Index